To see more of our books, visit us at:
www.PuppyDogsAndIceCream.com

LEARN

FUN FACTS

SIZE

WEIGHT

LOCATION

AGES 3-10

THE FANTASTIC WORLD OF
Marine Mammals

Dr. Iain Kerr, CEO of
Ocean Alliance

FUN FACTS
About Our
Seagoing Friends

About the Author

Everyone has heard about whales. We all know they are mystical and fascinating animals. Yet how many of us know how they live their extraordinary lives? Their talents range from communicating in the form of songs, to diving to unimaginable depths and hunting giant squid in the dark.

There are thought to be over **130 different species of marine mammals** alive on the planet today. The marine mammal group includes whales, dolphins, seals, sea otters, and manatees. But even polar bears are considered marine mammals because their food source and habitat are dependent on sea ice of the Arctic.

Marine mammals are actually very similar to humans. They are warm-blooded (allowing them to survive in colder climates), they breathe air (yes – whales and dolphins have to come to the surface to breathe!), and last - but not least - they also give birth to live young and produce milk to nurse their young.

Yet, for all these similarities, there are also enormous differences. Differences which we are only beginning to understand. It is my job to try and understand these differences.

Our eyes give us our primary picture of the world around us, allowing us to navigate, find food, and play games. Light does not travel well underwater, and so most marine mammals have evolved to live in a world of sound. Whales have taken this to the extreme. In fact, scientists believe that some whales can produce a more detailed picture of the environment around them using sound than we can see with our eyes! Imagine that - creating a clearer picture of the world around you - just with sound!

Why should we care about marine mammals?

Marine mammals play a crucial role in the ocean's ecosystem, they are of particular importance in fertilizing the ocean and encouraging primary productivity. If whales are healthy, then the oceans are healthy, then humans are healthy.

Whales are widely recognized as sentinels of ocean health: by studying them we can better understand the changes our oceans are going through.

As human's impact on this fragile planet continues to grow and grow, we push more and more species towards the edge of extinction. To me, this is desperately sad. All animals have a right to exist on this planet, not just us, and it is our responsibility to make sure that human impacts do not negatively affect them.

The challenges facing wildlife biologists and conservationists are more diverse than ever before, and protecting marine wildlife is no easy task.

Yet where there are problems, there are also opportunities. **Everyone on this planet has a role to play in protecting marine wildlife**. If you are interested in wildlife and conservation, my advice to you is to do what you love and then use that skill to help protect the natural world. If you like to write, then write about why the environment is important. If you like to draw, then draw pictures of whales to make people fall in love with them. If you like computers, then write code and software that can help scientists understand our oceans better.

I love studying whales. It has taken me to some of the most remote places on the planet, where I have seen enchanting and extraordinary animals behaving naturally in their own environment. I hope that you will now join me on a fun adventure as we seek to learn more about the mysteries of these incredible animals.

Dr. Iain Kerr
CEO of Ocean Alliance

Sea Otter

Enhydra lutris

FUN FACTS

Sea otters use tools, like rocks, to crack open food while floating on their backs in the water. While floating, there can be up to 1,000 individuals "rafting" together.

They have the thickest fur of any animal, containing between 600,000 to 1 million hair follicles per square inch

A strong, flat tail acts as a rudder while swimming

They use their whiskers to sense prey in hard to reach spaces while diving underwater

Where do they live?
Coasts along the Pacific Ocean

How big are they?
Male - 75 lbs = a Labrador Retriever
Female - 50 lbs
Male - 4.5 ft long, Female - 4 ft long

What do they eat?
Sea urchin, snails, clams, abalone, mussels, crabs, scallops, fish, octopus, worms, and squid

California Sea Lion

Zalophus californianus

FUN FACTS

Sea Lions are commonly found on rocks, cliffs, or bluffs because they can "walk" and "climb" with their flippers.

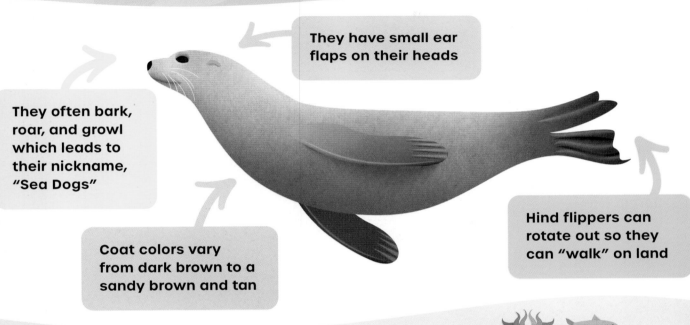

They have small ear flaps on their heads

They often bark, roar, and growl which leads to their nickname, "Sea Dogs"

Coat colors vary from dark brown to a sandy brown and tan

Hind flippers can rotate out so they can "walk" on land

Where do they live?
Along the coast of California

How big are they?
220 lbs = a panda bear
6 ft long

What do they eat?
Squid, anchovies, mackerel, rockfish, and sardines

Harbor Seal

Phoca vitulina

FUN FACTS

Their whiskers can sense a fish up to 115 ft away. Seals must scoot or shuffle to move on land, so they are commonly found on beaches, rocks, buoys, or ice blocks.

They do not have ear flaps

Primarily tan, silver, or blue-gray in coloration with dark spots

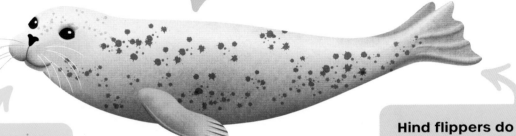

Hind flippers do not rotate out

They have short snouts like a dog

Where do they live?
Temperate coastal waters of North America, Europe, and Asia

How big are they?
130 lbs
5 ft long = a wolf

What do they eat?
Fish, shellfish, and crustaceans

Northern Elephant Seal

Mirounga angustirostris

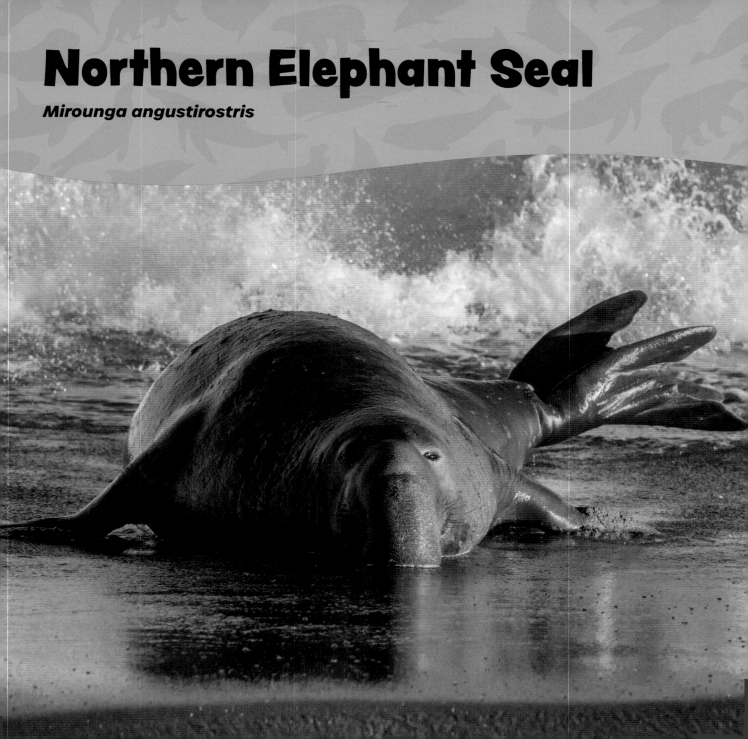

FUN FACTS

They can hold their breath for more than 100 minutes, and they can dive up to 5,000 ft deep. They're the second largest seals on the planet.

They have an inflatable nose called a proboscis that is used to resonate sound to warn or threaten other males

They are the largest member of the seal family

On land they move by scooting themselves onto a sandy beach

Males have an elongated nose that resembles an elephant's trunk

Where do they live?
Eastern and North Central Pacific Ocean

How big are they?
Male - 4,000 lbs = a car
Female - 1,000 lbs
Male - 13 ft long, Female - 10ft long

What do they eat?
Squid, fish, rays, and small sharks

Hooded Seal

Cystophora cristata

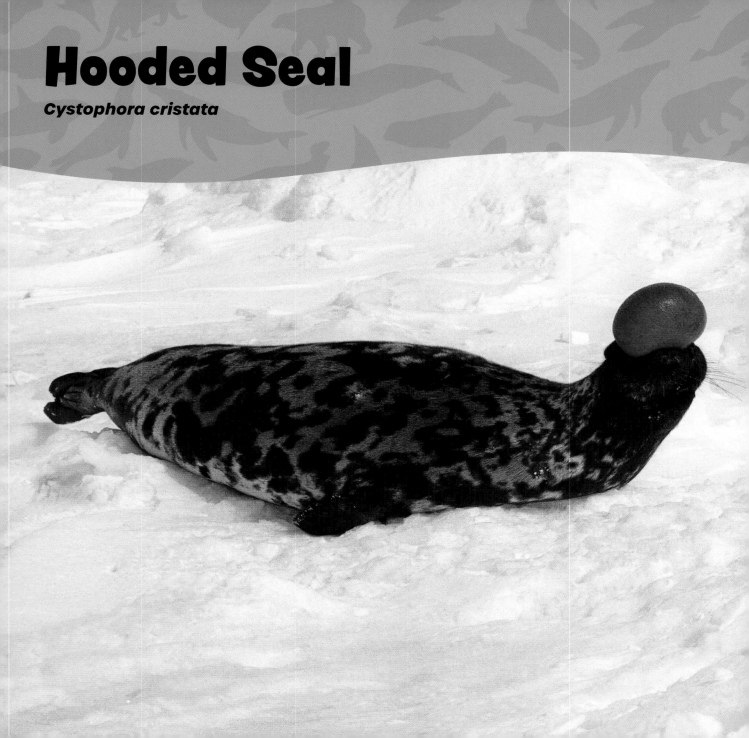

FUN FACTS

Hooded seal pups have the shortest weaning period of any mammal, lasting only 5 days. In that brief time, they double in size due to the rich fat content of their mother's milk which is crucial to their survival to produce an insulated layer of blubber.

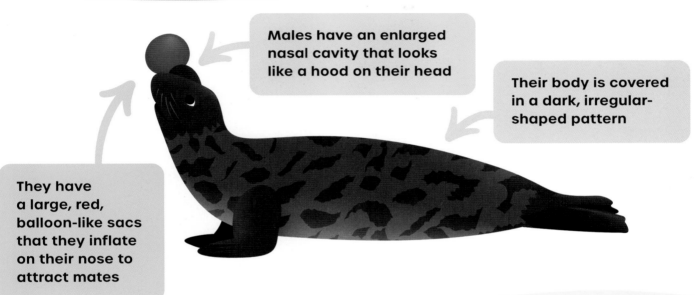

Males have an enlarged nasal cavity that looks like a hood on their head

Their body is covered in a dark, irregular-shaped pattern

They have a large, red, balloon-like sacs that they inflate on their nose to attract mates

Where do they live?
North Atlantic and Arctic Oceans

How big are they?
700 lbs = a tiger
8 ft long

What do they eat?
Squid, starfish, and mussels

Walrus

Odobenus rosmarus

FUN FACTS

They use their tusks to help crawl out of the water and onto ice, and also to protect themselves from predators. Mothers are very protective of their young and will even hug them tight while plunging into the water to avoid predators.

They have a mustache of whiskers around their mouth

Their fat and blubber is essential to their survival in extremely cold environments

Massive tusks protrude from their mouth that look like giant sabers

They have very short fur that covers most of their skin except for their flippers

Where do they live?
Arctic regions of the Pacific, Atlantic, and Arctic Oceans

How big are they?
2,200 lbs = a bull
12 ft long

What do they eat?
Crustaceans, octopus, and clams

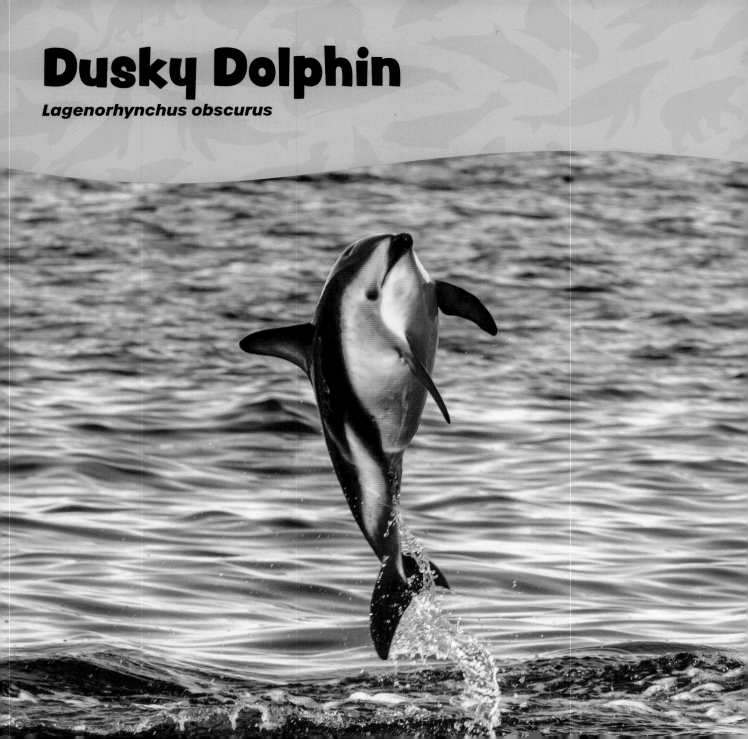

Dusky Dolphin

Lagenorhynchus obscurus

FUN FACTS

Dusky dolphins are extremely energetic and acrobatic dolphins. They will often be seen leaping out of the water in large groups in a playful manner.

They possess cone-shaped faces with a short, dark-colored beak

They have a similarly tall and curved dorsal fin compared to the common dolphin

Their acrobatic behavior is thought to be a form of communication, and may be used to coordinate attacks while hunting prey

They have a characteristic blaze of pale gray coloration along their side

Where do they live?
Off the coasts of New Zealand, South America, Southwestern Africa, and various oceanic islands

How big are they?
190 lbs
7 ft = height of a door

What do they eat?
Fish and squid

Common Dolphin

Delphinus delphis

FUN FACTS

These tactical hunters will corral large schools of fish into tight balls, known as "bait balls." They can also be playful, leaping out of the water while swimming in front of ships.

Dolphins are among the most intelligent animals on the planet

They have a tall, triangular dorsal fin that angles backwards and can have a white patch in the middle

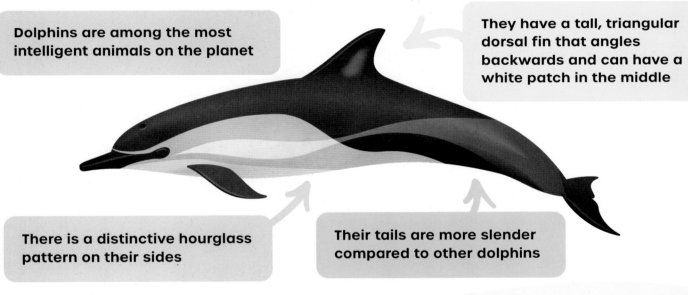

There is a distinctive hourglass pattern on their sides

Their tails are more slender compared to other dolphins

Where do they live?
Worldwide, primarily in the Atlantic and Pacific Oceans, but have also been found in the Indian Ocean

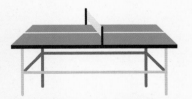

How big are they?
280 lbs
9 ft long = a ping pong table

What do they eat?
Fish, squid, crabs, and shrimp

Bottlenose Dolphin

Tursiops truncatus

FUN FACTS

Bottlenose dolphins have displayed tool use by carrying a sea sponge in the tip of their mouth. This acts as an armor to protect their nose from sharp rocks, stingrays, or other hazards while foraging food on the sea floor. Tool use is a credit to the dolphin's extreme intelligence.

They develop individualized whistle sounds to communicate with each other

Their dorsal fin is curved back and looks like a breaking wave

They have a short, thick snout shaped like the top of a bottle, giving them their name

Primarily light gray in color, they have a thicker body when compared to the common dolphin

Where do they live?
Worldwide except for the polar regions

How big are they?
1,400 lbs
12.5 ft long = a small car

What do they eat?
Fish, squid, crab, and shrimp

Spinner Dolphin

Stenella longirostris

FUN FACTS

They get their name from spinning in the air as they jump, and can even spin up to 7 times in one jump.

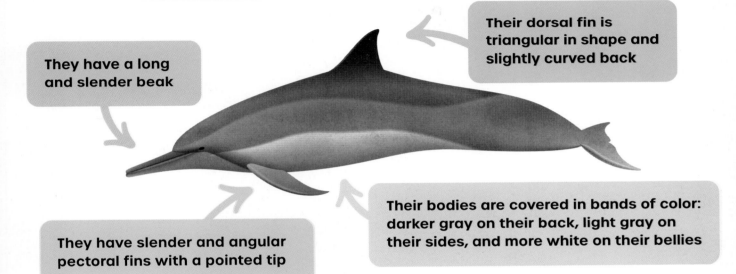

Their dorsal fin is triangular in shape and slightly curved back

They have a long and slender beak

Their bodies are covered in bands of color: darker gray on their back, light gray on their sides, and more white on their bellies

They have slender and angular pectoral fins with a pointed tip

Where do they live?
Throughout the world in tropical and warm-temperate waters but prefer deep ocean

How big are they?
170 lbs

7 ft long = a door

What do they eat?
Small fish, shrimp, and squid

Orca

Orcinus orca

FUN FACTS

They have complex behaviors that are learned and passed on to other members of the pod through teaching. They live in matriarchal groups often led by the grandmothers, and the offspring live their entire lives with their mother.

The nickname "killer whale" originated as "whale killer," and comes from early observations of them hunting larger whales

Their dorsal fin usually stands straight up, but some pods will have shorter and curved dorsal fins

Orcas use songs and whistles to communicate with each other

They can use their powerful tail fin to temporarily stun prey by slapping the surrounding water or the prey itself

Where do they live?
Throughout the world but primarily in Antarctica, Norway, and Alaska

How big are they?
Male - 12,000 lbs = an elephant
Female - 6,000 lbs
Male - 26 ft long, Female - 23 ft long

What do they eat?
Squid, fish, seals, sharks, whales, sea birds, walrus, and sea turtles

Dugong
Dugong dugon

FUN FACTS

Their closest relative is the elephant. Unlike manatees, dugongs do not venture into freshwater. Although they don't have many natural predators, dugongs are still threatened by illegal fishing.

Muzzle is angled downward and covered in short, dense bristles

More streamlined than manatees

Their fluke is more angular like a dolphin than the round paddle-like fluke of the manatee

Their upper jaw is strong so they can uproot grass from the seafloor

They have paddle-shaped flippers without nails

Where do they live?
Coastal waters of the Western Pacific Ocean and Indian Ocean

How big are they?
650 lbs = a brown bear
8 ft long

What do they eat?
Sea grass

Manatee

Trichechus

FUN FACTS

With their large paddle-like fluke, they are thought to have inspired mermaid legends. Even though they are most closely related to elephants, these grass-eating herbivores are commonly called "sea-cows".

Not as much of a down-turned snout as dugongs

They are more wide and round in the body than dugongs

Large, paddle-like fluke that is broad and round

They eat more than 10% of their weight a day in grass, which comes out to about 100 lbs

The tips of their flippers have blunt nails which remain from their ancestors who were four-legged land animals

Where do they live?
Gulf of Mexico and Atlantic Ocean

How big are they?
1,000 lbs = a horse
10 ft long

What do they eat?
Sea grass, algae, and mangrove leaves

Polar Bear

Ursus maritimus

Polar bears clean themselves by rolling in the snow. This is crucial to their survival by keeping their fur well-insulated for warmth, and to keep them camouflaged for hunting.

They will put their paws in front of their snout in order to blend into the snow while hunting

Polar bears are the largest land carnivore

Their wide paws provide a better grip and disperse their weight to traverse safely over ice

Polar bears will touch noses together to ask for food

Where do they live?
The Arctic

How big are they?
Male - 900 lbs, Female - 500 lbs
Male - 10 ft tall, = a basketball hoop
Female - 8 ft tall

What do they eat?
Ringed seals, bearded seals, and fish

Beluga Whale

Delphinapterus leucas

FUN FACTS

Their characteristic dome-shaped head has many unique qualities, but the most important is an enlarged echolocation chamber that aids them in finding breathing holes in the ice.

They can change the shape of their head by blowing air into it

No dorsal fin allows these arctic mammals to swim under ice with greater ease

Solid white through-out their body

They can swim backwards which is very useful while swimming in shallow waters

Where do they live?
Arctic Ocean

How big are they?
3,000 lbs = 2 cows
17 ft long

What do they eat?
Octopus, squid, crabs, shrimp, clams, snails, and sand-worms

Sperm Whale

Physeter macrocephalus

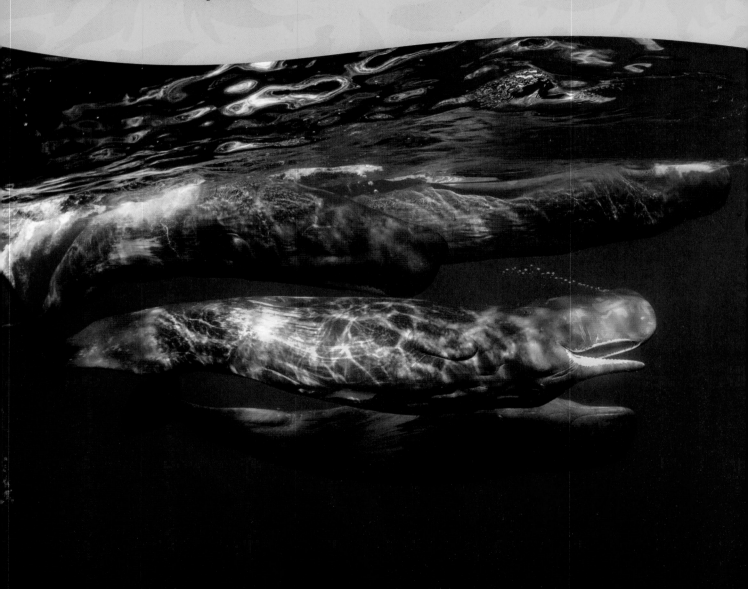

FUN FACTS

Sperm whales are known for diving to extreme depths of 8,000 feet for 100 minutes to hunt.

Their massive heads take up about 1/3 of their entire body length

They are the only living large whale that has a blow-hole located on the left side of their head instead of the center

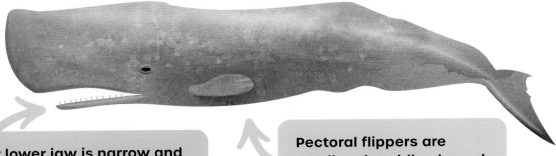

Their lower jaw is narrow and filled with teeth, making them the largest toothed predator

Pectoral flippers are small and paddle-shaped

Where do they live?
Circumglobal in all Oceans

How big are they?
90,000 lbs
52 ft long = a semi truck

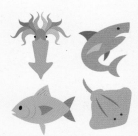

What do they eat?
Squid, sharks, skates, and fish found in deep water

Humpback Whale

Megaptera novaeangliae

FUN FACTS

Humpback whales have one of the longest migrations of any animal, traveling up to 5,000 miles each year. They will also sing to each other as a form of communication.

Can blow bubbles or use sounds to disorient or direct prey

Commonly seen jumping out of the water and smacking the surface with their pectoral fins or tails

They eat up to 3,000 lbs of food a day

They have large pectoral fins that can be up to 8 ft long

Where do they live?
Every ocean

How big are they?
66,000 lbs = a fire truck
Male - 46 ft long, Female - 52 ft long

What do they eat?
Krill and small fish

Blue Whale

Balaenoptera musculus

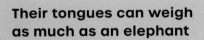
FUN FACTS

Blue whales are the largest animal to have ever lived. Their low frequency calls can be heard more than 5,000 miles away. This makes them one of the loudest animals on the planet, even if we can't hear them.

Their tongues can weigh as much as an elephant

They can hold up to 11,000 lbs of water in their mouth at a time

Adults can eat up to 80,000 lbs of krill per day

Instead of teeth, these whales have thick baleen bristles to filter out their tiny prey

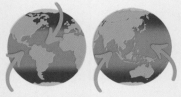

Where do they live?
All oceans except the arctic

How big are they?
330,000 lbs
Male - 79 ft long = an airliner
Female - 85 ft long

What do they eat?
Krill: tiny crustaceans only growing to a few inches in length

Photograph Credits and Copyrights.

CLAIM YOUR FREE GIFT!

Visit

PDICBooks.com/Gift

Thank you for purchasing
The Fantastic World of Marine Mammals,
and welcome to the
Puppy Dogs & Ice Cream family.

We're certain you're going to love
the little gift we've prepared for you
at the website above.